THE LITTLE BOOK OF
MARY

THE LITTLE BOOK OF
MARY

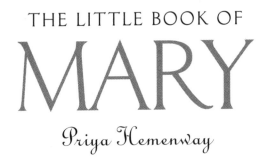

Priya Hemenway

BARNES
& NOBLE
BOOKS

NEW YORK

This edition published by Barnes & Noble, Inc.,
by arrangement with The Book Laboratory® Inc.

The Little Book of Mary
©2004 The Book Laboratory® Inc.

Design by Amy Ray
Cover by Amy Ray and Bullet Liongson

2004 Barnes & Noble Books
M 10 9 8 7 6 5 4 3 2 1

ISBN: 0-7607-5451-9

Printed in Singapore

Contents

Introduction

Mary, the mother of Jesus, has been revered for centuries as a woman particularly graced by God. She is endowed with qualities of love and benediction that have endeared her to generations of Christian worshippers, and she is a figure of feminine grace and blessed love who is venerated for her compassion as well as for her relationship to Christ.

For many, Mary is the welcomed portent of salvation. Through her body the Word of God was given human form, and she is called *Theotokos*, a Greek word meaning "carrier or bearer of God in her womb." To others she is more simply the devoted mother who gave birth to Christ, the Son of God, and is a divine expression of motherly love whose femininity helps balance an otherwise masculine Trinity.

Mary is known by many names and has been seen myriad times in a variety of forms: She has inspired the devout and cured the sick and is a blessing to those who call her name. To those not so devoted to Christian articles of faith, Mary is a symbol of fertility who links human needs with divine providence.

In this little book we will consider some of the history, legends, tales, and prayers that surround Mary. We will take a look at the scriptures that describe her for Christian believers and examine lesser-known information that relates her to more ancient cults. Some of the many names that represent Mary divide the book into sections, and the religious art that has glorified her for centuries serves to say what words cannot.

The first part of the book describes Mary as she is portrayed in the scriptures. The first section is called *Blessed Mother*. Here the most familiar story of Mary is recounted—the story that comes to us from the New Testament of the Bible. This is a story that has been told countless times, and it is here that Mary appears as the virgin maiden who conceived the child Jesus through a miraculous conception with the Holy Spirit. As scholars have recently indicated, the Gospels were written many years after the death of Christ. The authors, like others in antiquity, were probably not as concerned with historical facts as they were with enhancing the spiritual essence of beliefs that were to guide a newly formed religion for centuries.

The second section is called *Daughter of Zion* and explains the background of many of the concepts that were used to describe Mary in the New Testament

and in symbols and thoughts that have developed around the scriptures. This is followed by a look at details of Mary's life that come from apocryphal sources in the section, *Virgin Mary*, and at some of the many articles of Marian worship in the section, *Queen of Heaven*.

In *Mystical Rose*, symbols that relate Mary to the natural world are described, and Mary becomes less married to prayer and scripture and is brought into the realm of everyday remembrance. In the Middle Ages flowers became signatures of her presence and legends developed that united fantasy with belief to create images whose usage continues into the present.

The final section, *Mother of Mercy*, portrays Mary as the extraordinary feminine figure who appears in apparitions. She represents the feminine aspect of God's love, and has made numerous appearances. She cares for the humble and the innocent and helps protect those who pray to her.

Mary shows herself differently to everyone. She is a beacon of faith and a symbol of love. She embodies the fertile Word of God that through her womb was made human, and she portrays the transformation that devotion makes possible. Mary is, like most women, a mystery who is best known through love.

Blessed Mother

The story of Mary, the Blessed Mother of Jesus, is told in the New Testament of the Bible. For centuries the few details of Mary that had been remembered were related as part of the story of Jesus, her son. Her unique relationship with him and his Father has made of Mary a figure who is both heavenly and temporal. Mary, in her role as Blessed Mother is the virgin who gave birth to the Son of God and she is often called Mother of God.

The writers of the four Gospels—Matthew, Mark, Luke and John—do not say much about Mary. However, over the centuries the little that was remembered has flowered magnificently in our great treasure of religious art and music. The episodes of the annunciation, the nativity, and the crucifixion and of her own ascension have been rendered time and time again, reminding us continuously of the heavenly aspects of Mary.

In this section we will revisit the details of Mary's life that are recounted in the Gospels of Matthew and Luke, along with some of the episodes that are closely related to her and without which her story would be incomplete.

The Annunciation

We are told in the Gospel of Luke that Mary was a young virgin who had grown up in Nazareth and was espoused to a carpenter named Joseph. One day while she was alone in the house she was startled by the appearance of the angel Gabriel who announced himself to her with the words, "Greetings, you who are highly favored! The Lord is with you."

Mary was afraid and seeing this, Gabriel calmed her and told her that she has been blessed by God. "You will conceive a son in your womb, and his name shall be Jesus." He went on to explain to Mary that her child was to be conceived through the grace of the Holy Spirit and not through Joseph. "He will be known as the Son of God."

Mary may have been confused by this, but she humbly bowed her head in submission to the will of God saying, "Behold, I am the Lord's servant. May it be as you have said."

With this the angel departed.

Joseph

The ancient prophets of Israel had long ago announced the coming of a Messiah. He was to be of the line of David, who had united the tribes of Israel, and was to be born in Bethlehem. Joseph, the carpenter to whom Mary was betrothed, was a direct descendant of King David. When he learned of Mary's pregnancy he was shocked, for he knew he was not the father. Not being sure what to do, Matthew tells us that he fell into a fitful sleep from which he was suddenly awakened by an angel.

Gabriel told Joseph not to be perturbed and to take Mary as his wife. He explained to Joseph that Mary had been blessed. "That which is conceived in her is of the Holy Ghost. Mary will give birth to a son who you will name Jesus, and he will become a savior of the people." Hearing these words Joseph remembered the ancient prophecies that foretold of a virgin who would bring forth a son. He would be called Emmanuel which means "God is with us."

Having woken from his sleep Joseph knew that he must take Mary as his wife and that he must take the greatest care of her, for in her womb Mary carried the divine child who was to become a Savior to the people of Israel.

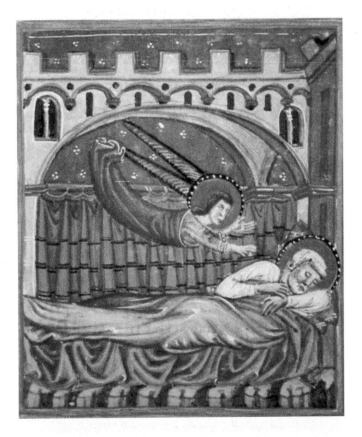

Zacharias and Elizabeth

These heavenly revelations to Mary and Joseph happened six months after another miraculous event—the conception of a child in the womb of Mary's cousin Elizabeth.

Zacharias and Elizabeth were an old, devout, and childless couple who lived in the hills of Judea. According to Jewish beliefs at the time, a woman's infertility was an indication of God's displeasure, and so Elizabeth lived with the stigma of divine reproach.

Zacharias was a priest; and one day while he was burning incense in the Temple, an angel appeared beside the altar. Zacharias was greatly troubled at this, but the angel, who was Gabriel, told him not to be afraid. "Your prayers have been heard, and your wife Elizabeth will bear a son. You will call him John."

Gabriel went on, "You will experience great joy and gladness at the birth of John, for there are many who will rejoice in his words in the days to come. He will be a great man in the sight of the Lord and he will be filled with the spirit of God. He will turn the children of Israel towards the Lord their God. He will follow in the footsteps of the prophets and will make the people ready for the coming of the Lord."

Zacharias said to the angel, "How can this be? I am an old man, and my wife is so far advanced in years that this seems impossible."

The angel answered, "I am Gabriel, a messenger of God. He sent me to inform you of what is happening so that you would understand. Now you will be struck dumb, and you will not be able to speak until all this has come to pass. It will be as I have spoken, and your trust in God will be your blessing."

A great crowd of people had been waiting outside the Temple for Zacharias to finish burning the incense. They were surprised that he had taken so long, and when he stumbled out, they immediately sensed that he had seen a vision in the Temple. He tried with his hands to explain what had happened for, as the angel had said, he remained speechless.

Having left the temple Zacharias returned home to his wife. Elizabeth soon conceived a child. Clearly her prayers were answered and God had blessed her.

Elizabeth was in the sixth month of her pregnancy when the angel Gabriel appeared to Mary announcing the miraculous conception of a child in her womb. Before departing the angel had further announced that her cousin Elizabeth, who was reputedly barren, had conceived a son in her old age, so Mary went to visit her cousin. Upon entering the house she called out Elizabeth's name and ran to embrace her. As she did so the child in Elizabeth's womb leaped as if in recognition of the child that Mary carried. Elizabeth was filled with wonder and, as if inspired by a great understanding of what had happened, she said out loud, "Blessed you are among women, and blessed is the fruit of your womb." She went on to ask of Mary, "How is it that the mother of my Lord has come to visit me? I don't understand; but with the voice of your salutation ringing in my ears, the child in my womb has leaped for joy."

Mary, overcome by all the wonderful events burst into song with a prayer of joy and thanksgiving that was to be sung for generations to follow. The prayer she sang is recorded in the Gospel of Luke. It is called *The Magnificat.*

THE MAGNIFICAT

My soul doth magnify the Lord,

And my spirit hath rejoiced in God my Savior.

Because he hath regarded the humility of his handmaid;

for behold from henceforth all generations shall call me blessed.

Because he that is mighty hath done great things to me,

and holy is his name.

And his mercy is from generation unto generations,

to them that fear him.

He hath showed might with his arm;

he hath scattered the proud in the conceit of their hearts.

He hath put down the mighty from their seat, and hath exalted the humble.

He hath filled the hungry with good things; and the rich he hath sent empty away.

He hath received Israel his servant, being mindful of his mercy:

As he spoke to our fathers, to Abraham and to his seed forever.

John the Baptist

As the angel had announced, Elizabeth gave birth to a son; and as was the custom, eight days after his birth he was taken to the Temple to be circumcised. The priests were about to name the child Zacharias after his father; but Elizabeth burst out, "No, he shall be called John."

The priests were surprised at this for Zacharias had no relatives named John, and they turned to the father for validation. Zacharias asked for a writing tablet with which he confirmed what Elizabeth had said. "His name is John."

Then, all of a sudden, Zacharias found he was able to speak. He praised God and went on to bless his son with a prophecy. "You will become a prophet of the Highest; and you will go before the coming Lord to prepare his way. You will announce to his people their salvation through his remission of their sins—for he will give light to those who sit in darkness and will guide their feet in the way of peace."

Word of this prophecy began to spread around the country; and the people of Israel began to wonder, and their hearts were filled with anticipation.

The Nativity of Jesus in Bethlehem

Meanwhile, according to the Gospel of Luke a decree had gone out from Caesar Augustus that heavy taxes were to be imposed on all the Roman provinces. Every male Israelite was to return to the city of his birth to pay his due; and so it was that Joseph took Mary out of Nazareth to Bethlehem, in the province of Judea, to be taxed.

And it was in Bethlehem—the city of David—that Mary gave birth to her child. As has so often been repeated, she wrapped him in swaddling clothes, and laid him in a manger, because there was no room for them in the inn.

In nearby fields there were some shepherds, watching over their flocks, and suddenly there appeared before them an angel. The shepherds were terrified but the angel put them at ease and said to them, "Fear not: for I bring you good tidings of great joy, which shall be to all people."

As they began to relax and quiet down, the angel continued with a proclamation of the wonderful news, "Unto you is born this day, in the city of David, a Savior who is Christ the Lord."

The shepherds expressed their joy and made ready to go and see the miracle. They were further told, "And this will be a sign for you: You will find the child wrapped in swaddling clothes, lying in a manger."

And suddenly there appeared in the sky a heavenly host of angels, praising God, and saying, "Glory to God in the highest, and on earth peace, good will toward men."

When the angels had disappeared the shepherds looked at one another and decided to go to Bethlehem immediately to see what had happened there. When they arrived, they found Mary, with Joseph nearby, and the infant lying in a manger.

After bestowing their best wishes upon the child, the shepherds left and went back to their village. They began to talk of what had happened and all those who heard their tale were fascinated by the events, and word of what had happened spread quickly.

Mary was quiet and her heart was filled with gratitude.

The Prophecy of Simeon

At the ceremony of his circumcision that took place eight days later, the child was given the name of Jesus. Following Jewish law, as the first-born male, he was consecrated to God and a sacrifice of two turtle-doves was made for him.

There was at the time a man named Simeon who had had a vision which revealed to him that he would not die until he had set eyes on the Messiah. Simeon went to the Temple when Jesus was brought there by his parents. Once the ceremony was over, he took the child in his arms and prayed, "Master, let your servant go in peace. As has been promised to me, my eyes have seen the salvation you have promised—a light of revelation for the gentiles and glory for your people Israel." Mary and Joseph stood by and Simeon blessed them and said quietly to Mary, "Your son is destined to be opposed; there are those who will want to destroy him; and with this a sword will pierce your soul too, but through your sorrow the hearts of many will be opened."

Soon after this a prophetess named Anna, a widow who served in the temple, came forward and also gave thanks. She too picked up the babe and spoke of the coming redemption of mankind through the child she held in her arms.

The Three Wise Men

The Gospel of Matthew goes on to recount the story of the three wise men. It tells us that it wasn't long before news of the miraculous events surrounding the birth of Mary's child reached King Herod. Three wise men from the East came to his court and asked where they could find the newborn child, the King of the Jews. They said they had seen his star in the night sky and that they had come to worship him.

When Herod heard this, he was troubled and he gathered his chief priests and demanded that they tell him where the child was. These men told Herod that the prophets of old had told of a child that would be born in Bethlehem.

Herod then called the wise men and asked them more about the star they had seen. He told them to go to Bethlehem and to find the child. "When you have found him, bring word to me that I too may go and worship him." With this the wise men left and as they went towards Bethlehem, a bright star guided them to the place where the young child was. The wise men entered the stable and finding the child and his mother, Mary, they fell to their knees in prayer.

They opened up the treasures they had brought and presented the child with gifts of gold, frankincense and myrrh.

Warned by God in a dream that they should not return to Herod, the wise men went home by another route. When they had gone, an angel appeared to Joseph in a dream, saying, "Get up and take the young child and his mother with you. Flee into Egypt and wait there until I bring you word, for Herod will seek the child out and will destroy him."

When Herod realized his order to the wise men had been mocked he was furious. In a story not borne out in historical fact, Matthew tells us that Herod ordered his soldiers to kill all the children under two years old who lived in the lands near Bethlehem. A great mourning arose throughout the lands—the sound of which is known as the lament of Rachel who wept for her children and who would not be comforted, because they are not.

When Herod finally died, an angel again appeared in a dream to Joseph and told him to return to Israel with the young child and his mother. The family returned to the city of Nazareth; and there the young child grew. He was strong in spirit and was filled with wisdom. The grace of God was upon him.

The Child in the Temple

Joseph and Mary went to the Temple in Jerusalem every year at the feast of the Passover and when Jesus was twelve they took him with them. After the feast they began the journey back to Nazareth while, unbeknownst to them, Jesus stayed behind in Jerusalem. They traveled for the better part of a day before they realized he was not with them, and when they discovered his absence they went back to Jerusalem and sought him out.

It was only after three days that they found him in the Temple. There he was, sitting in the midst of all the learned men, listening to them and asking questions. Those who stood nearby were astonished by his understanding. When Mary and Joseph saw him, they were shocked. Mary asked him why he had not come with them and Jesus answered that "I must do my Father's business." Not understanding this response, Mary turned it over in her heart and the family returned home to Nazareth.

As the child grew older his wisdom increased and he was loved by all who met him for he was filled with grace and had a gentle heart.

John the Baptist

As the years passed Jesus and his cousin John grew older. Little is known of either of them until they were both around thirty years old. By this time John was fulfilling his father's prophecy and was preparing the way for the coming Christ. He left behind the priestly ways of his father and went into the desert wilderness of Judea where he lived on locusts and wild honey for many years.

Having at some time understood clearly what he was to do, he began to preach a new message. He told the people that, contrary to the belief they held, simply being Israelites was no longer enough to guarantee their salvation in the eyes of God. They must, he said, repent for their sins and through a new rite of baptism renounce who they had been and embrace a change of heart. The rite of baptism that he performed became an initiation and those who were thus submerged in water would emerge ready to embrace the teachings of the new Messiah. They would be, he told them, as newborn infants. Having died to the old, they would be born into a new life.

In the years since the births of both John and Jesus, word of the miracles had spread and great expectations about the coming Messiah had grown. Many people came to hear John preach and to be baptized. They asked him whether or not he was the Christ. To this John answered them saying, "While it is true that I baptize you into new life with water, one far mightier than I is coming. The ties of his shoes I am not worthy to unloose. He will baptize you with the Holy Ghost and with fire."

One day Jesus appeared before John on the banks of the Jordan, ready to be baptized. When John saw the young man approaching he called out loudly to him, asking him to stop. "It is I who needs to be baptized by you; how is it that you come to me?"

Jesus explained simply that this is how things are meant to be. John consented and baptized him.

Upon being baptized, Jesus emerged from the water and walked toward the bank of the river. As John watched, the skies appeared to open and the Spirit of God descended upon him like a dove. A voice from heaven said, "This is my Son, whom I love; with him I am well pleased."

The Wedding of Cana

The baptism of Jesus by John the Baptist was the commencement of the ministry of Jesus. With this the child ceased to be the son of Mary and began to emerge as the Messiah. With a deepening understanding, the Blessed Mother became a disciple of her own son. In the story of the Wedding of Cana, Mary is mentioned as she prompts him into his new role.

Jesus found the first of his disciples and had been invited to bring them to a wedding. Mary was also at the wedding, and at one point she noticed that the wine for the guests had run out. She said to Jesus, "They have no more wine."

"Dear woman, why do you involve me?" Jesus replied, "My time has not yet come." Mary went over to the servants and told them to do whatever Jesus should tell them to do. Nearby there were six large stone water jars, and after a while Jesus went to the servants and asked them to fill the jars with water. They filled them to the brim, and then he told them to draw some of the water out and serve it to the guests. When they tasted the wine the guests had no idea that it had recently been water. They did not know where the drink had come from—but the servants who had drawn the water knew.

Who is My Mother?

Jesus began to move from place to place, speaking to people wherever they gathered. One day his mother approached him along with some other members of his family. They wanted to speak with Jesus. A man in the crowd motioned toward them and said to Jesus, "Look, your mother and your family have come. They have something to say."

"Who is my mother? and who my family?" Holding his hand out towards his disciples, Jesus then said, "Look! Here is my mother and my family! All those who come close to me are my family."

Another time when he was speaking to a crowd, Mary and others in the family again came close. They were standing at the doorway to the room in which he stood and someone came up to Jesus and told him.

"My mother and my brothers and sisters are these who hear the word of God and are moved by it." With these words Jesus made it very clear that he was the Son of God. He indicated by this that all ties to the past must be severed and having dedicated himself to those who openly received his teaching, he spoke with the authority of a man who was redesigning old ways of thinking so that God could be seen in a new light.

Mary, the mother of Jesus, had been called "blessed" by God. The great transformation that happened to her when Gabriel announced the conception of a child in her womb is unknown to us. In some sense she can be likened to an empty vessel who received the word of God with humility and graciousness. She allowed the Spirit of God to move through her and was a witness to the miracle of Christ that was created in her womb.

While she does not appear at all in the stories of Jesus' short ministry in Galilee until his death in Jerusalem, we might suppose that Mary became a disciple or that she followed him wherever she could. If she was not actually present, then she certainly kept herself informed of everything that happened to him.

Jesus was as dear to Mary as any son is to his mother, but he was also a great teacher and his words probably held a profound meaning for her, for Mary's heart had opened to Jesus as the Savior long before he began to teach. Her humility and her deep love for God would have served her well in the difficult role she played and as she witnessed the events of his life.

The Crucifixion

The last time we see Mary in the stories of the New Testament is as a witness to the crucifixion in Jerusalem. According to the Gospel of John she was one of the very few who came close and stood near to the cross upon which Jesus had been nailed. Beside her were three other women who also loved him dearly: his mother's sister, Mary the wife of Clopas, and Mary Magdalene.

Jesus, looking down, saw his mother weeping. Nearby stood the disciple John. Jesus said gently to Mary, indicating John, "Woman, behold, your son!" Then he said to John, "Behold, your mother!" From this time on, John took care of Mary as a son would take care of his mother.

The Bible further tells us that after the crucifixion Mary went to pray with the other disciples. Invoking the spirit of their Master to remain among them, at them at the celebration of Pentecost, they were rewarded a short time thereafter, when Jesus miraculously appeared to give his final instructions.

Daughter of Zion

Though little is recorded about Mary in the New Testament, many stories were told about her in the early days of the Church. Symbolic images developed out of Old Testament legends and myths sprang up from apocryphal sources. Concepts evolved that were later captured in art and music, and over the centuries Mary evolved into a figure of enormous spiritual significance.

In the obscure town of Bethlehem in the province of Judea the long-awaited Messiah of the Israelites was born to a young virgin woman named Mary. Through her role in fulfilling the prophecies of the Old Testament she became known as the Daughter of Zion. As Daughter of Zion, she was not only the mother of Christ, she also gave birth to a great flowering of the deep relationship that existed for thousands of years between God and the people of Israel.

In the Gospels, the only existing records in the Bible that tell us anything specific about Mary, we are told that she was a woman of extraordinary humility. She was clearly a woman who was capable of bearing tremendous sorrows and who was also capable of transforming those sorrows into love.

Mary sought no revenge for the death of her son. Rather, she is remembered as a woman of compassion and forgiveness.

Although the Gospels say so little about her, looking back through the Old Testament it is clear that a variety of references to her had been made in the past. Many prophets had spoken about the coming Messiah and the woman who was to bring him into the world. Symbols had developed that described the vehicle through which he would be known or how he would emerge. Although it may not have been clear exactly how she would be recognized, or when she would appear, it was absolutely expected that she would come and that she would give birth to the coming Messiah, the salvation of the people of Israel. Through the body of a woman the Messiah would arrive and then they would realize their redemption.

To understand more exactly how the symbols and ideas developed it is helpful to look back at some of the concepts established in the Old Testament. Mary, the Virgin and Blessed Mother is also the Daughter of Zion. Zion is an early name for Jerusalem, and Daughter of Zion carries connotations of both royal splendor and of motherhood. Daughter of Zion evokes an image of the most holy of shrines and of a place of refuge.

Jerusalem

The earliest reference to Zion comes in the account of David's conquest of Jerusalem. Israel's greatest king and one of the most beloved figures in the Bible, David ushered into the country a period of great spiritual and political stability.

The holy site of Urushalim, as it was originally called, had been under the control of the Jebusites, one of the several groups of people living in the land of Canaan that the Israelites eventually conquered. Archeologists have suggested that a fortress called the "stronghold of Zion" may have been located on the crest of a hill in one corner of the settlement. After David's victory, he renamed this stronghold "the city of David."

Because of its physical features and the presence of a fresh-water spring, the site was of strategic importance to the Israelites, and David made it the capital of his newly established kingdom. Over time the city of Jerusalem grew to include the Temple mount. At the dedication of the Temple, David's son and heir, Solomon, had the Ark of the Covenant brought up to the Temple from "the city of David, which is Zion."

Arc of the Covenant

The Ark of the Covenant was one of the most important objects in the stories of the Hebrew Bible. It was a small wooden chest that symbolically represented the presence of God in Israel. Its construction was associated with the covenant that God made with his people at Mount Sinai in the days of Moses. It contained the manna (bread from heaven), stone tablets of the ten commandments (the word of God), and the staff of Aaron (a symbol of Israel's high priesthood), and was kept in the Tabernacle.

Originally a moveable meeting tent where Moses and others would go, over time the Tabernacle became a temple where God could be consulted. Symbolically it became the place where God was perceived to be present among his people, a place where he met and communicated with them. Zion eventually became a word to denote not only the city of David but the Tabernacle, the dwelling place of God.

As the dwelling place of God, or *Yahweh* as he is called in the Hebrew Bible, Zion was the site of the throne of God, and was portrayed as a lofty peak extending into the sky, and became the meeting point of heaven and earth.

Zion

It shall come to pass, that the mountain of the house of the Lord shall be established in the top of the mountains, and it shall be exalted above the hills; and people shall flow unto it. And many nations shall come, and say, Come, and let us go up to the mountain of the Lord, and to the house of the God of Jacob; and he will teach us of his ways, and we will walk in his paths: for the law shall go forth of Zion, and the word of the Lord from Jerusalem. (MICAH 4:1-2)

Because God reigned in Zion as both king and as defender of the people of Israel, Zion became a symbol of security and refuge, especially for the poor. These concepts eventually gave rise to a notion of Zion's inviolability. The people of Jerusalem believed that God would protect His throne against Assyrian and Bablyonian threats and thus Zion became that which would endure even beyond Jerusalem's destruction.

After Jerusalem and the Temple were destroyed in 587/586 B.C., hope for the future was sometimes expressed in terms of the restoration of Zion, and Zion further carried the connotation of a mother who would carry new life in her womb.

Other Old Testament Symbols

Besides the phrase "Daughter of Zion," there are several prophecies in the Old Testament that refer to Mary and establish related symbols that have long been used to depict her in art. The earliest of these comes from the vision of Jacob's ladder. Jacob, the son of Isaac, had a dream in which he saw a ladder that reached up to Heaven. It had angels ascending and descending along its rungs and has been used to describe the method by which God would enter the physical world—a role that Mary clearly embodied.

Another Old Testament symbol used to describe Mary is the burning bush that was seen by Moses. An angel of God appeared in the flames of the bush that burned but was not consumed. This bush has been likened to the purity of Mary and a common understanding of the symbol is that through giving birth to the Son of God she remained pure and did not lose her virginity.

The virginity of Mary is understood by some to refer to the purity of her heart and not to a physical state. In this case, the burning bush is a very appropriate symbol that describes the flame of love in her heart as a fire that could not be extinguished.

Tree of Jesse

During the Middle Ages, the Old Testament prophecy that the coming Messiah would spring from the family of Jesse, the father of David, was interpreted visually as a genealogical tree. God had promised David that his Kingdom would last forever and that through him and his seed God would save His people and bless the world.

Jesse is often depicted as reclining at the base of the tree that rises out of his loins and the ancestors of Christ are shown emerging from the branches of the tree that culminates in the Virgin and Child.

The genealogical diagram of Christ's lineage from David's father Jesse was inspired by Isaiah's prophecy that "There will come forth a rod out of the root of Jesse and a flower will rise up out of his root." The rod (*virga* in Latin) was interpreted as the Virgin Mary and the flower as Jesus. In some pictures, the root of the tree grows out of either the burning bush or the ladder of Jacob.

Virgin Mary

The four Gospels of the Bible record very few incidents from the life of Mary. Nothing is said about her parentage, her own nativity, or her childhood. All the information we have about these events comes to us from the early tradition of the Church, which was recorded in the middle of the second century (about A.D. 175) in the apocryphal book called *The Protoevangelium of Saint James*.

The apocryphal books are early Christian writings that tell us about certain events from the lives of Jesus and Mary that are not included in the Gospels. Although the apocryphal writings are not recognized by the Catholic Church as authentic works, much of what they relate does in fact belong to the tradition of the primitive Church.

From *The Protoevagelium of Saint James* we learn that Mary's parents were named Joachim and Anna, and that they were righteous and greatly devoted to God. Joachim was descended from the royal house of David and Anna came from the priestly line of Aaron. Their one great sorrow was that they had no children. According to the traditions of their faith when God blessed His chosen people, He promised to bless them with numerous offspring. Thus, among the Jews, childlessness was considered to be a sign of God's rejection.

One day an angel appeared before Joachim and said "God has heard your prayer and your wife Anna will conceive and give birth to a daughter, whose nativity will become joy for the entire world." When the child arrived and her sex was announced, there was great celebration and thanksgiving among those who had been told.

The feast of the Nativity of the Blessed Virgin Mary is one of the oldest Marian festivals, although we don't know for sure when it first appeared. According to tradition, Saint Helen, the mother of Emperor Constantine built a basilica in Jerusalem in about 330 and dedicated it to Mary's nativity. As happened with other Marian feasts in those early days, the nativity of the Virgin Mary was celebrated only locally and without any major solemnity.

It was not until the seventh century that the celebration of Mary's nativity spread to Rome. During the following centuries the feast day spread throughout the entire West and was finally established on September 8.

Presentation of the Holy Virgin into the Temple

After the angel's announcement Joachim and Anna had promised to dedicate their child to God, and when Mary was three years old they brought her to the Temple. Friends and relatives gathered together and formed a procession that brought her to the foot of the stairs leading up to the Temple. Then the child Mary walked all by herself to the top of the stairs and was met by the High Priest, Zacharias. Inspired by the Holy Spirit, he declared, "The Lord will surely magnify your name in every generation. Through you He will manifest His redemption to the sons of Israel." Then Zacharias set her down on the third step of the altar, and those who were present saw a certain grace descend upon her. She danced and the air was filled with joy.

Mary remained in the Temple for twelve years until the council of priests gathered to decide what needed to be done for her. They asked Zacharias to pray for an answer, and so he went to the inner temple and prayed. He saw an angel who told him to gather together the men of the village and to look for a sign from God. This was done, and when a dove alighted upon Joseph's head Zacharias said to Joseph, "You have been chosen to take into your keeping the virgin of the Lord."

Queen of Heaven

The theme of the heavenly coronation that made Mary the Queen of Heaven has often been represented in religious art and music. It is related to her being assumed into Heaven where she reigns in glory next to her Divine Son. The theme Queen of Heaven has evolved out of a long history of beliefs, dogmas, and papal declarations and its roots lie back in the days of beliefs and practices that pre-date Christianity.

Devotion to Mary began in the first few centuries after the crucifixion, when the new religiousness first spread to Europe. Christians of all denominations have venerated her since that time, but with slight differences. Whereas many branches of Christianity see Mary largely as an historical figure, Catholicism focuses on her as a living entity who intercedes on behalf of humanity. In this section we will look at some of the different forms that devotion to Mary, the Queen of Heaven has taken.

The central role of Mary in the Catholic Church is reflected in the fact that many churches contain side altars dedicated to her. She is also celebrated through major religious pilgrimage sites where it is claimed apparitions or appearances have occurred. Her miraculous powers to help those who pray are granted to her by God, and her many intercessions on the part of humanity are ultimately the result of God's love and omnipotence.

Throughout the history of the world, sites associated with one religion have often been reused by another religion that followed it. This was a way of reinforcing the new religion in the hearts of people who had been converted, allowing them to continue with the festivals and rites that were essential to their harvests and to their social codes.

In the early days of Christianity, when this very new religiousness was first beginning to spread through Europe, older earth-based gods, goddesses, and their festivals were assimilated into it. The result was that characteristics of deities of different faiths became intermingled with characteristics of saints and major figures in Christianity. The moon and stars, symbols of Diana, the Greco-Roman goddess of hunting were associated with Mary, and she was frequently referred to as Stella Maris—Star of the Sea. A Roman festival of purification at winter's end became the Festival of the Purification of the Blessed Virgin.

The Rosary

The Rosary is the most famous of all forms of prayer to Mary. It is prayed using a set of prayer beads as a way of remembering God and to contemplate the mystery of life. There are twenty mysteries, specific to the life of Mary and Jesus, that are reflected upon when the Rosary is prayed. These are divided into the five Joyful Mysteries, the five Luminous Mysteries, the five Sorrowful Mysteries, and the five Glorious Mysteries.

The word Rosary means "Crown of Roses," and over the centuries Mary has appeared to several people to remind them of the importance of repeating its prayers. Time and time again she has stressed the significance of praying the Rosary as a simple way of practicing faith.

Just as the rose is taken to be the queen of flowers, so the Rosary is the rose of all devotions. It is considered a perfect prayer, because within it lies the story of salvation. A short prayer called the Hail Mary is the basic prayer of the Rosary, and with each repetition, believers hand Mary a symbolic rose. Each complete Rosary makes a crown of roses.

History of the Rosary

Legend tells us that the Rosary first appeared in 1214 when Saint Dominic was attempting to convert the Albigensians to Christianity. He was so dejected by his failure that he retired to a cave in the wilderness. After three days of fasting and prayer, he collapsed, exhausted, and had a vision in which Mary appeared to him accompanied by three queens and fifty maidens.

She raised him up, kissed him, and then told him that "thundering" against heresy was not going to help, but rather that a gentle remedy against sickness was required. "Therefore, if you would preach successfully, preach my Psalter." She showed him a Rosary made of beads that smelled of roses, which, the legend says, she had brought from her rose garden in Paradise. Then she vanished.

Dominic arose, comforted, and burning with the zeal of conversion. He made straight for the local cathedral, and as he entered unseen angels rang the bells to gather the people together. When they were assembled, Saint Dominic began to preach.

He had barely begun his sermon when an appalling storm broke out. The earth shook, the sky was darkened, and there was so much thunder and lightning that everyone was terribly afraid. Their fear grew even greater when they looked at a picture of Mary that hung in a prominent place. They saw her raise her arms to heaven three times to call down God's vengeance upon them if they failed to be converted, to amend their lives, and seek the protection of the Christian God.

The storm finally quieted down when Saint Dominic said a prayer, and once the air had cleared he went on with his preaching. So fervently and compellingly did he explain the importance and value of the Rosary that almost everyone embraced it. They renounced their beliefs as false beliefs and in a very short time they began leading Christian lives.

Inspired by the Holy Spirit, and instructed by the Blessed Virgin, Saint Dominic preached the Rosary for the rest of his life. He preached it by his example as well as by his sermons, wherever he went and to whomever he could speak. Rich and poor, educated and uneducated, young and old, people began to repeat the prayers he taught them.

The Prayer of Hail Mary

The Hail Mary is the most familiar of all the prayers used by the Church in honor of Mary. It is sometimes called the "Angelical Salutation" and is also known in its Latin form of "Ave Maria."

The Prayer of Hail Mary consists of three parts. The first is the salutation, "Hail Mary full of grace, the Lord is with thee, blessed art thou among women." This phrase repeats the words used by the angel Gabriel to announce the miracle of the coming Christ.

The second part, "and blessed is the fruit of thy womb" comes from the divinely inspired greeting of Elizabeth when Mary arrived at her door, and is a way of giving thanks to God for the miraculous gift that was borne through Mary's womb.

The prayer ends with the petition "Holy Mary, Mother of God, pray for us sinners now and at the hour of our death. Amen." This part of the prayer asserts the belief that Mary can act as an intercessionary on behalf of those who desire to reconcile with God.

Mysteries of the Rosary

For hundreds of years the Rosary was made up of fifteen "mysteries." These were seen to be the most significant events in the life of Jesus that are recounted in the four Gospels and they were divided into three series. Each series was repeated on a certain day and comprised five mysteries. They are the Joyful Mysteries (recited on Mondays and Saturdays), the Sorrowful Mysteries (Tuesdays and Fridays), and the Glorious Mysteries (Wednesdays and Sundays.)

The Joyful Mysteries draw our attention to the beginning of Christ's life on earth. The Sorrowful Mysteries help us realize the immense love Jesus had for humanity. His suffering and death are a reminder of how, through our own daily lives, we can be transformed. The Glorious Mysteries teach us about the resurrection that is possible through prayer and meditation.

On Oct. 16, 2002, Pope John Paul II formulated five new mysteries, which he called the Mysteries of Light, or the Luminous Mysteries. These are contemplated on Thursdays and are the events through which we are led on a journey of transformation. As the light glows brighter, the darkness in the world around us diminishes.

The Joyful Mysteries

The Annunciation (Humility)
The angel Gabriel appears to Mary, announcing she is to be the Mother of God.

The Visitation (Charity)
Elizabeth greets Mary: "Blessed you are among women and blessed is the fruit of your womb!"

The Nativity (Poverty)
Mary gives birth to the Redeemer of the World.

The Presentation (Obedience)
The Blessed Mother presents the child Jesus in the Temple.

Finding in the Temple (Piety)
The Blessed Mother finds Jesus in the Temple.

The Sorrowful Mysteries

The Agony in the Garden (Contrition)
At Gethsemane, Jesus prays as he contemplates the sins of the world.

The Scourging at the Pillar (Purity)
Jesus is cruelly scourged until his body can bear no more.

Crowning with Thorns (Courage)
A crown of thorns is placed on the head of Jesus.

Carrying of the Cross (Patience)
Jesus carries the heavy cross upon his shoulders to Calvary.

The Crucifixion (Self-Denial)
Jesus is nailed to the cross and dies after hours of agony.

The Glorious Mysteries

The Resurrection (Faith)
Jesus rises, glorious and immortal, three days after his death.

The Ascension (Hope)
Jesus ascends into Heaven forty days after his resurrection.

Descent of the Holy Spirit (Love)
The Holy Spirit descends upon Mary and the Apostles.

The Assumption (Eternal Happiness)
The Blessed Mother is united with her divine son in heaven.

The Coronation (Devotion to Mary)
Mary is gloriously crowned Queen of Heaven and earth.

The Luminous Mysteries

The Baptism of Christ in the Jordan by John the Baptist
The heavens open, and the voice of the Father declares Jesus the beloved son.

The Wedding Feast at Cana
The first of the signs of Jesus' grace, when he changes water into wine thanks to the intervention of Mary, the first among believers.

The Announcement of the Kingdom
Jesus proclaims the coming of the kingdom of God in which all those who draw near to Him in humble trust will be forgiven their sins.

The Transfiguration
The glory of God shines forth from the face of Christ as he commands the astonished Apostles to "listen to him."

The Institution of the Eucharist
Christ offers his body and blood and himself as a sacrifice.

Feasts and Prayers of Mary

Mary is celebrated on several Catholic Feast days throughout the year. The Month of May is both named for and dedicated to Mary and October is dedicated to the Rosary.

January 1	Solemnity of Mary
January 8	Our Lady of Prompt Succor
February 2	Presentation of the Lord
February 1	Our Lady of Lourdes
March 25	Annunciation
May 31	Visitation
June 27	Our Mother of Perpetual Help
July 16	Our Lady of Mount Carmel
August 15	Assumption
August 22	Queenship of Mary
September 8	Birth of Mary
September 15	Our Lady of Sorrows
October 7	Our Lady of the Rosary
November 21	Presentation of the Blessed Virgin Mary
December 8	Immaculate Conception by her mother, Saint Anne
December 12	Our Lady of Guadalupe

Music

Prayers to Mary and verses that sing her praise have been set to music since medieval times and are known as Antiphons of the Blessed Virgin Mary. Many of these were set in the early musical form known as plainsong, and several sixteenth-century composers wrote settings of the antiphons in what was a particularly rich period of Church music. One particularly famous setting of a Marian theme is Monteverdi's *Vespers of the Virgin Mary*, which was written in 1610.

The Magnificat of Johann Sebastian Bach (1685–1750) is an acknowledged masterpiece. The eighteenth- and early nineteenth-century composers Haydn (1732–1809), Mozart (1756–91), and Schubert (1797–1828) wrote scores of settings of such favorite devotions as the *Ave Maria* and *Salve Regina*. In the Romantic period, Berlioz (1803–69) composed a beautiful oratorio called *L'Enfance du Christ*.

Marian devotional music plays a significant part in the Mass that is said in Christian Churches. Hymn books are full of verses that praise her blessedness and her purity, and call upon her to remember believers before God.

The Immaculate Conception

The doctrine of the Immaculate Conception was officially defined by Pope Pius IX in 1854. It declares that Mary was conceived by her mother Saint Anne and her father, Saint Joachim, without original sin. The festival associated with the Immaculate Conception is celebrated annually on December 8.

Because many people have been confused, it is important to understand that the doctrine of the Immaculate Conception does not refer to Christ's conception in Mary's womb.

The Immaculate Conception refers to Mary. It says that Anna and Joachim conceived her in the normal way, but that she was born without original sin. By the grace of God her sanctity was preserved in order that she might give birth to the Messiah.

The Assumption

It is believed by Catholics that at the end of her life on earth, Mary was "assumed," body and soul, into heaven. This teaching was espoused by Saint Gregory of Tours in the sixth century. An earlier tradition had it that all the Apostles witnessed her death, but that when her tomb was opened years later it was found to be empty. On November 1, 1950, Pope Pius XII declared the Assumption of the Blessed Virgin to be an article of faith. It is celebrated annually on August 15.

The doctrine of the Assumption says that at the end of her life on earth Mary was assumed into heaven just as the Prophets Enoch, Elijah, and perhaps others had been before her. It is necessary to keep in mind that, according to the doctrine, the Assumption does not imply that Mary "ascended" into heaven. Christ, by his own power, ascended into heaven. Mary was assumed or taken up into heaven by God. She didn't do it under her own power.

Christians believe that finally all good people will be raised into heaven and rendered immaculate. As the first person to welcome the good news of Jesus, Mary has received the blessing that will one day be given to all.

Mystical Rose

For nearly two millennia Mary, the mother of Jesus, has been the predominant female figure in Western culture. In religion, in sacred art and music, and as the inspiration for the construction of some of the most magnificent cathedrals, she has been given numerous names: Queen of Mercy and Peace, Joy of Israel, Gate of Heaven, Refuge of Sinners, and Holy Mother of God are among many names for Mary.

While a great variety of symbols have been incorporated into the art and poetry that in some way describes her, those of the flower gardens are most widespread. Before the rise of Christianity, flowers were associated with many pagan deities. In fact the whole of the natural world was inhabited by the spirit of godliness in different forms, and when Christianity superceded the pagan, the flowers were "christened" and many were rededicated to Mary.

The faithful saw Mary's attributes in the herbs and flowers growing around them and named many plants after her. Legends about the flowers developed as people sought to connect them with events from Mary's life.

Roses and lilies in particular became Mary's flowers. A legend from the second century says that when her tomb was opened to show Thomas that her body had been assumed into heaven, it was filled with both these flowers.

Rose legends reached a peak in the twelfth century and included the following: The Rosa Alba turned pink when Mary blushed at the angel's annunciation, the Christmas Rose sprang up to provide flowers for a poor shepherd who had no gift for the Infant Jesus, and the Rose of Jericho marked the spot where the Holy Family rested during their Flight into Egypt.

Hundreds of other flowers and herbs were named after Mary. The violet was associated with humility and became known as Our Lady's Modesty. It was said to have blossomed when the angel Gabriel appeared to Mary to announce the miraculous conception of a child in her womb. Spurs of columbine that look like slippers received the name Our Lady's Shoes. They were said to have sprung up where Mary's feet touched the earth when she was on her way to visit Elizabeth. Because the little flowers also resemble tiny doves they came to represent the Holy Spirit and also symbolized the innocence of Mary. Snowdrops became a symbol of Mary's purity and were called the Flower of Purification because they bloomed at the time of the Feast of the Purification

in February. In Italy and other European countries, the statue of Mary was removed from the altar on that day and snowdrops were strewn in its place. The marigold was called Mary's Gold by early Christians who placed the flowers around statues of Mary, offering the blossoms in place of coins. There is a legend that during the Flight into Egypt the Holy Family was accosted by a band of thieves who took Mary's purse. When they opened the purse, marigolds fell out.

In Sicily it is said that the Madonna's Juniper Bush opened its branches to shelter the Holy Family when Herod's pursuing soldiers drew near them as they fled to Egypt. The rosemary bush and clematis were also said to have sheltered them during the Flight. The blossoms of sea-pink or thrift are said to have formed cushions for Mary to sit on when she rested during the journey and became known as Our Lady's Cushion. The fragrance of rosemary arose after Mary hung her linens to dry on its branches. Lavender also was said to have received its scent after Mary laid Jesus' clothes on the plant to dry. It was called Mary's Drying Plant.

Thistle was called Our Lady's Thistle. The leaves of the plant are said to have become spotted when drops of milk fell on them while Mary was nursing

Jesus. Leaves of the spotted cowslip of Jerusalem also became spotted when drops of Mary's milk fell on them. Lily of the Valley was known as Mary's Tears. It is said that when Mary cried at the Cross, her tears turned into this flower. The strawberry was called Fruitful Virgin. It was said that a mother who had lost a child would not eat strawberries on that day, for if she did, Mary would ask the child to stand aside when it arrived in heaven, saying, "Your mother has eaten your share."

The harebell or blue wood hyacinth was called Our Lady's Thimble and tendrils of the honeysuckle plant became Our Lady's Fingers, while the foxglove plant, with its glove-like blossoms, became Our Lady's Glove. There is a legend that says Jesus hung the pendant-like blooms of the fuchsia plant on his mother's ears and the shrub was called Our Lady's Ear-drop. Impatiens is also known as Our Lady's Earrings.

There are many herbs also named after Mary. Spearmint was known as Our Lady's Mint. Marjoran was Mother of God's Flower. Bee balm and lemon balm were both called Sweet Mary. Catnip was Mary's Nettle. Sage was Mary's shawl. Dandelion was known as Mary's Bitter Sorrow. Mints and pennyroyal were said to have been used in the manger.

Besides flowers, there are several other symbols that have been associated with Mary for centuries. Most notable are the colors in which she is dressed—blue and white being the ones that are most usually used. In the symbolism of colors, white stands for purity and blue for wisdom. From references in the Old Testament we have symbols of the burning bush, the Arc of the Covenant, and the Tree of Jesse. She is often associated with an apple or a snake, portraying a relationship of Mary with Eve.

Stars are another interesting symbol often associated with Mary. At the time of the birth of Jesus, Sirius, the Star in the East, and Orion, called "The Three Kings" by oriental astronomers, were both in the night sky. The constellation of Virgo (the Virgin) was rising in the east. The brightest and largest star in the constellation of Virgo is called Spica—the "ear of corn." The ear of corn is an ancient sign of fertility and Mary often holds one in her hand.

The constellation of Virgo is composed of three stars in the shape of a chalice or cup—perhaps the Holy Grail. The chalice in Christian symbolism holds the wine or blood of Jesus and is the repository of the sacred and the holy.

Mother of Mercy

Biblical Christianity is a very masculine affair in which God the Father, Son, and Holy Spirit are perceived as male characters—although an old tradition speaks of the Holy Spirit as feminine. Many of the older pagan religions that Christianity replaced were female-based and revered mother goddesses who were associated with fertility and the seasons. Some people think that from the very earliest days of the Church, the veneration of Mary has filled a void and has provided a necessary balance of male and female.

It is interesting in this respect to consider the tradition of Black Madonnas. The worship of Black Madonnas clearly predates Christianity and in its earliest forms prevailed throughout the ancient world.

Historians such as Gerald Massey recognize that the statue of the Egyptian Goddess Isis with her child Horus in her arms was the first Madonna and Child and that they were renamed Mary and Jesus when Europe was Christianized. He writes that "Roman legions carried a figure of black Isis holding the black infant Horus all over Europe where shrines were established to her. So holy and venerate were these shrines that when Christianity invaded Europe, the figures of Isis holding Horus were not destroyed but turned into figures of the Black Madonna and Child. Today these are still among the holiest shrines in Catholic Europe."

Titles such as The Great Mother were originally attributed to Isis. The word "Madonna" itself comes from the Latin, *Mater Domina*, a title used for Isis. The month of May, which was dedicated to the pagan Virgin Mothers, became the month of Mary, the Christian Virgin.

Also interesting concerning the color of the Black Madonnas, is the fact that in Aramaic, the language of Jesus, the word "black" means "sorrowful." Aramaic was a language of highly descriptive idioms, and through this inference Mary was linked to Isis who, in her search for Osiris, was described as "sorrowing."

In the early years of Christianity's spread through Europe, statues of Mary often replaced statues of earlier goddesses. It is possible that the earliest Black Madonnas were replacements for the earth goddesses who had been converted to Christianity—goddesses like Ceres, the Roman goddess of agricultural fertility whose Greek equivalent, Demeter, derives from *Ge-meter* or Earth

Mother. In this respect it is also interesting that the best fertile soil is black in color. The blacker it is, the more suited it is for agriculture.

In the roots of Christianity as we understand them today, the concept of Earth Mother is also apparent in the story of Adam and Eve. Many people see a parallel between the Adam of Genesis and Christ in the New Testament in which Christ is called the "New Adam." In this view Mary parallels the earth and is called the "New Eve."

Saint Augustine (354–430) wrote that "Virgin Mary represents the earth and Jesus is of the earth born." The symbolism of this statement relates to the rite of baptism that John the Baptism initiated and that Jesus often referred to. Mary is not only likened to earth as the source of fertility and new life, she is also the agent of death and rebirth for "everything comes from earth and returns to it."

Apparitions of Mary

Besides the relationship of Mary to early earth goddesses, there is another aspect of her that is particular to her feminine roots and the mystery of life that the goddess represents. Unlike the male figures of Father, Son, and Holy Ghost, Mary has made numerous appearances or apparitions all over the world, and she has been credited over the centuries with numerous miracles of healing and conversion. Shrines and churches have been built where she has been seen and they have become the focus of pilgrimages by the devout.

The characteristics of Mary's apparitions have remained fairly consistent no matter where or when they took place. She usually appears in a globe of pure white light, dressed in a long dress with a shawl or head cover. Her feet are usually surrounded by a mist or cloud, and she occassionally is seen holding her Son in her arms.

A number of her appearances have been preceded by unusual phenomena such as lightning or thunder from a clear sky, apparitions of angelic beings or clouds of unusual shapes, and religious significance such as a cross or a doorway as well as other inexplicable events.

Descriptions of a few of Mary's appearances throughout Christian history are related on the following pages. Whether believable or unbelievable they are testament to the trust that ancient feminine deities and symbols have always instilled in the heart of those who believe in them.

The first stories of Mary's apparitions began in A.D. 40 and she has appeared at irregular intervals throughout the two thousand years since then. Appealing to the innocent and to those in need, Mary has usually declared herself by name and often with a specific request to build a shrine or church in her memory. She has always spoken in the local dialect of those whom she has appeared before and has consistently offered proof that her apparitions are real.

Our Lady of the Pillar
Saragossa, Spain (ca. 40 AD)

After the crucifixion, resurrection, and ascension of Jesus, his Apostles began spreading his message throughout Israel and the Roman Empire. One of these Apostles was called James (the Greater), and he reportedly traveled as far west as Spain to the village of Saragossa where he became disheartened because of the failure of his mission. One day while he was deep in prayer Mary appeared to him and gave him a small wooden statue of herself and a piece of jasper wood and instructed him to build a church in her honor.

A year later James built a small chapel which became the first Church dedicated to the honor of Mary. Afterward James returned to Jerusalem, where he was executed by Herod Agrippa in about A.D. 44. Some of his disciples later returned his body to Spain. The local queen, observed several miracles performed by James' disciples and converted to Christianity. She permitted James' body to be buried in a local field. Eight centuries later, a cathedral was erected near his gravesite, a spot that was discovered by a local hermit when he noticed an unusual star formation. The site for the cathedral was called Compostella (starry field), and it is a major pilgrimage site.

Our Lady of Walsingham
Walsingham, England (ca. 1061)

Lady Richeldis de Faverches was a widow who lived in Walsingham, England. In a series of visions, Mary showed her the house in Nazareth where the angel Gabriel had announced to her the birth of Jesus. She asked Lady de Faverches to build a replica of the house and to dedicate it to the Annunciation.

A church was later constructed around the house to protect it from the elements, and during the Middle Ages, Walsingham became one of the most popular pilgrimage sites in Europe. King Henry VIII made three pilgrimages there before breaking with the Catholic Church and forming the Church of England—at which time he ordered the destruction of all Catholic shrines and places of religious worship. The Walsingham church and house were destroyed in the rampage that followed.

In the 1920s Walsingham Holy House was rebuilt. A small chapel called the Slipper Chapel (for those who took off their slippers to enter) had managed to escape the destruction. It became the Catholic Shrine of Our Lady in England. Both sites have become active pilgrimage sites once again.

Our Lady of Mount Carmel
Aylesford, England (1251)

The original Mount Carmel in Israel was the dwelling-place of the first and greatest of the Jewish prophets, Elijah, who defeated the pagan prophets of Baal. It is said that he lived there in a cave in the ninth century B.C., and many stories are told of him: He called down fire from heaven to dismay his enemies; he was fed by ravens; he saw a cloud "no bigger than a man's hand" which brought rain to ease a drought in Israel and which contained a vision of the Daughter of Zion; and at the end he did not die but was taken up into the presence of God in a chariot of fire.

John the Baptist of Saint Alexis, who built the first monastery at Mount Carmel, said that God revealed the dogma of the Immaculate Conception to Elijah in a cloud. He also told a story of a visit Mary made to Elijah's cave when she was a young girl and said that Jesus took shelter there with Mary and Joseph on their return to Nazareth after the escape into Egypt.

The visions of Elijah inspired the initiation of the Carmelite Order during the twelfth century. The Order grew out of the hermit tradition in which men and women adopted a life of solitude and prayer in sacred locations in the Holy Land. The first Carmelite monks were devoted to Mary and made her their patroness. When the Crusades made life dangerous in the Middle East, they left the Holy Land and settled in various places in the West. The few monks who remained behind were massacred by invading Muslims.

Many years later a certain Friar Stock from Aylesford, England, was visited by Mary while on a pilgrimage to the Holy Land. She entrusted him with a brown scapular (two pieces of woolen cloth that are embroidered with an outline of Our Lady of Mount Carmel, tied together by string, and worn over the shoulders.) "My beloved son, use this scapular for your Order. It is a special sign of privilege, which I have fashioned for you and for all those who will honor me in the future as Our Lady of Mount Carmel. Those who die clothed with this scapular will be preserved from eternal fire. It is a badge of salvation and a shield in times of danger. It is also a pledge of peace and special protection, until the end of time."

After this apparition the scapular became one of the most widely used religious symbols of personal dedication to the mission of Mary. Friar Stock went on to establish Carmelite communities in England, France and Italy.

The Black Madonna
Czestochowa, Poland (1382)

The Black Madonna is a legendary painting of the Madonna and Christ Child that it is said was painted by Saint Luke on a tabletop built by the carpenter Jesus. The legend goes that while he was painting, Mary told Luke about the events in the life of Jesus and that these tales were eventually incorporated into Luke's Gospel.

The painting disappeared until A.D. 326 when Saint Helen located it in Jerusalem while on a pilgrimage there. She gave it to her son, Constantine, who had a shrine built in Constantinople to house it. In a critical battle with the Saracens, the portrait was hung from the walls that surrounded the city and was credited with the victory.

The painting was later owned by Charlemagne, who subsequently presented it to Prince Leo of Ruthenia with whom it remained until an invasion in the eleventh century. As a result of Leo's prayers to the Virgin, a misty darkness descended on the enemy troops. In their confusion the invading soldiers began attacking one another and Ruthenia was saved.

In the fourteenth century, the painting was transferred to the Mount of Light in Poland in response to a request the Virgin made in a dream. In 1382, when invading Tartars attacked the fortress of Prince Ladislaus, an arrow hit the painting and lodged in the throat of the Madonna. Fearing that he and the painting might fall to the enemy, the Prince escaped during the night and fled to the town of Czestochowa where the painting was installed in a church. A monastery was later built to ensure the picture's safety, but it was looted by invading Hussites who wanted the portrait for themselves. One of the looters twice struck it with his sword. Before he could strike a third blow, he fell to the floor writhing in agony and died. Both sword cuts and the arrow wound are still visible on the art.

In 1655 Poland was almost entirely overrun by the Swedish army, but the monks of the monastery successfully defended the portrait during a siege. The Polish army was able to drive the invaders out, and the Lady of Czestochowa became a symbol of national unity and was crowned Queen of Poland. Over the centuries there have been many reports of miraculous events and spontaneous healings in the presence of the portrait. Some say that it is called the Black Madonna because of the soot residue that discolors the painting—the result of centuries of votive lights and candles burning in front of it.

Our Lady of Guadalupe
Guadalupe, Mexico (1531)

Juan Diego was an Aztec Indian who had been converted to Christianity during the Spanish conquest of Mexico. One day he was walking through the country to a chapel near Tepayac Hill when he encountered a beautiful woman surrounded by a ball of light as bright as the sun. Speaking in his native tongue, the lady identified herself, "My dear son, I love you and I want you to know that I am the Virgin Mary. I would like a church to be built here so that your people may experience my compassion. All those who come to ask for my help in their work and in their sorrows will feel my heart. I will see their tears; I will console them, and they will be at peace. So run now to Tenochtitlan and tell the Bishop all that you have seen and heard."

Juan, who had never been to Tenochtitlan, immediately responded to Mary's request. He went to the palace of the Bishop and requested a meeting. He was kept waiting for several hours, and when the Bishop finally appeared he told Juan only that he would consider the request of the Lady. Juan was disappointed and was overcome by feelings of unworthiness. He returned to the hill where he had first met Mary and found her waiting. He implored her to send someone else, but she said to him, "My son, there are many I could send. But you are the one I have chosen."

She told him to return the next day and repeat her request to the Bishop. After another long wait, Juan met with the Bishop who requested that Juan ask the Lady to provide a sign as proof of who she was. Juan dutifully returned to the hill and told Mary of the Bishop's request. She told him "Do not fear. The Bishop will have his sign. Come back here tomorrow. Peace, my son."

Unfortunately, Juan was not able to return the next day, for his uncle had become mortally ill. When the old man was ready to die, Juan went off to find a priest. He had to pass Tepayac Hill to get to one, and as he was passing, he found Mary waiting. "Do not be distressed, my son. You are under my shadow of protection. Your uncle will not die now, and there is no reason for you to engage a priest. His health is being restored as I speak. Go cut some flowers from the top of the hill and bring them to me."

Although it was freezing out, Juan obeyed Mary's instructions and went to the top of the hill. There he found a full bloom of Castilian roses. He cut a great armful and carried them back to Mary who said to him as she rearranged the roses, "This bunch of flowers is the sign I am sending to the Bishop. Tell him that I request his greatest efforts to complete a church on this spot. Show these flowers to no one but the Bishop. You are my trusted ambassador. This time the Bishop will believe everything you tell him."

At the palace, Juan went before the Bishop and opened his jacket to let the flowers fall out. However, it wasn't the beauty of the roses that caused the Bishop to fall to his knees. Attached to Juan's coat was an image of the Blessed Virgin precisely as Juan had described her.

When he returned to his village that evening, Juan found his uncle had been completely cured. He said he had met a young woman who told him that she had just sent Juan to Tenochtitlan with a picture of herself. She said, "Call me and call my image Santa Maria de Guadalupe."

Within six years, six million Aztecs had converted to Catholicism. The image that mysteriously appeared on Juan's coat has been subjected to smoke from fires and candles, and water from floods and torrential downpours. In 1921, a bomb was planted on an altar underneath it by anti-clerical forces. The picture remained untouched!

Our Lady of Lourdes
Lourdes, France (1858)

Bernadette Soubirous was a poor and very sickly fourteen-year-old girl who lived in the Pyrenees at a time of great turmoil in France. One day she went, with her sister Marie and another friend to a nearby river to gather firewood. Marie and her friend crossed the river to search the other side while Bernadette stayed on dry land. Suddenly she heard a loud noise that seemed to come from a nearby grotto known as Massabielle. At the mouth of the grotto a rosebush appeared. Then, from deep inside the grotto she saw a golden-colored cloud appear. Soon afterward a beautiful lady came to the entrance of the opening just above the rosebush. The Lady smiled at Bernadette and motioned for her to come close. Bernadette lost all fear and fell to her knees in prayer. A little while later, the Lady slowly withdrew to the interior of the grotto and disappeared.

Over a six-month period Bernadette experienced eighteen visitations from Mary. She had no idea who the Lady was until the last apparition. During one apparition Mary instructed Bernadette to dig a hole in the ground and to drink and bathe in it. The hole later turned into a spring of water, which Mary promised would heal all who came to its waters. Mary asked Bernadette to tell the local pastor, Cure Peyramale, to have a chapel built in honor of her appearances there. The Cure accused Bernadette of lying about the apparitions and told her to find out from the Lady just who she was and to demand that she perform a miracle by making the rosebush in the grotto bloom.

On March 25th, the Feast of the Annunciation, Mary answered the Cure's request. She told Bernadette, who she was: "*Que soy era Immaculado Conception*" (I am the Immaculate Conception). With these words she confirmed a recent declaration from the pope concerning the Immaculate Conception. It was highly unlikely that this could have been known by Bernadette, an uneducated fourteen-year-old in rural France who had received only the most rudimentary religious education.

The apparitions at Lourdes were declared authentic in 1862, and the spot rapidly became one of the world's major pilgrimage sites. Thousands have been cured from a variety of illnesses, both physical and spiritual, and a clinic to support the millions of pilgrims who come to Lourdes operates to this day. Bernadette returned to a life of obscurity. She was declared a saint in 1933 because of her dedication to a life of simplicity and service.

The Virgin of Fatima
Portugal (1917)

Portugal in the early twentieth century was suffering from tremendous political upheaval and economic bankruptcy. It was a time for radical solutions, and in 1911 Alfonso Costa, the head of state, promised as part of the cure to wipe out Catholicism "within two generations."

In the spring of 1916, Lucia Dos Santos age 9, and her two cousins, Francisco and Jacinta Marto, ages 8 and 6 respectively, were tending their sheep in a meadow outside the small hamlet of Fatima. It started raining, and the children ran into a cave. Eventually the rain stopped, and the children sat down in the cave to eat their lunch and say the Rosary when, suddenly a strong wind came up and a great white light appeared. In the middle of the light they saw a man who said to them, "Don't be afraid! I am the Angel of Peace. Pray with me!" The children, imitating the angel, knelt on the ground and repeated his words. When they had finished he told them to pray in this fashion every day.

A few months later the angel appeared again. This time he again told them to offer their prayers daily. "Jesus and Mary have plans for you, and you will have to sacrifice yourselves." The children asked him in what way they must sacrifice themselves and the angel replied, "Make everything you do a sacrifice, and offer yourselves willingly as a petition for the conversion of all sinners. If you do this, peace will come to your country. I am the Guardian Angel of Portugal."

A third apparition of the angel occurred in the autumn. This time he held in his hand a chalice over which hung a Host. The angel knelt and taught the children a new prayer that he urged them to remember and to repeat daily. Then he rose, took the Host, and gave it to Lucia, and gave the contents of the chalice to Jacinta and Francisco.

On Sunday May 13, 1917 the children were pasturing their flock at the Cova da Iria, which was about a mile from their homes. Suddenly a bright light pierced the air. The children thought that they had better head home in case it should start to rain. As they descended the hill another flash of light took them by surprise, and panicky with fear they huddled together and looked around. There, standing above a shrub, was a lady dressed in white and surrounded by a beautiful light. She spoke to them saying, "Don't be afraid. I will not harm you."

The children wondered at her and wanted to know where she had come from. "I am from heaven," she replied. "I have come to ask you to return to this spot for six consecutive months, on the thirteenth day, at this same hour. I will tell you later who I am and what I want." Then she told them, "You will have to suffer, but the grace of God will be your comfort." She opened her hands with a loving gesture and urged them to "Recite the Rosary every day to obtain the peace for the world and the end of the war." Then she disappeared.

The children returned to Cova da Iria on June 13, accompanied by about fifty people. The Lady appeared again and told them that Francisco and Jacinta would soon be taken to heaven, but that Lucia would remain on earth.

On July 13 they again saw the vision. This time Lucia said, "I would like to ask you to tell us who you are, and to make a miracle for the crowd to believe that you appear." The Lady said that she would do so on October 13th. "Sacrifice yourselves for the sinners of the world, and pray often. When my request is granted, Russia will be converted and there will be peace. If this does not happen, her ways will be scattered throughout the world, provoking wars and persecution of the Church. The good will be martyred, the Holy Father will suffer, and many nations will be destroyed."

On August 13 the civil authorities took the children into custody and interrogated them, telling each child separately that the others had been boiled in oil for their lies. None of them changed the story, and they were released. The Lady appeared to them and said she would keep her promise to perform the October miracle. She then asked for a chapel to be built at Cova da Iria.

On September 13 thousands had gathered in the valley at midday. Although the Lady appeared and spoke with the children, the rest saw nothing.

On October 13 an even greater crowd gathered. The day was dark and oppressive. After speaking with the children and asking them to continue their prayers the Lady said, "I am the Lady of the Rosary. Pray the Rosary every day and the war will end." Then she opened her hands and launched a ray of light in the direction of the sun. Lucy shouted to the people that they should look at the sun.

The rain suddenly stopped and a bright light appeared. The sun began to move and to project bands of color that lit and colored the clouds, the sky, the trees, and the crowd. It stayed still for a few moments and then suddenly it moved again seeming as if it was about to fall headlong onto the crowd. Terrified, they fell to their knees and begged for mercy. Meanwhile the children saw the Lady dressed like the white of the sun with a blue cope. Saint Joseph and the Christ Child stood with her, and Jesus blessed the world.

A few days later a major Lisbon newspaper reported the event. "At one o'clock in the afternoon, midday by the sun, the rain stopped. The sky, pearly gray in color, illuminated the vast arid landscape with a strange light. The sun had a transparent gauzy veil so that eyes could easily be fixed upon it. The gray mother-of-pearl tone turned into a sheet of silver which broke up as the clouds were torn apart and the silver sun, enveloped in the same gauzy gray light, was seen to whirl and turn in the circle of broken clouds. A cry went up from every mouth and people fell to their knees on the muddy ground. The light turned a beautiful blue as if it had come through the stained glass windows of a cathedral and spread itself over the people who knelt with outstretched hands. The blue faded slowly and then the light seemed to pass through yellow glass. Yellow rays fell upon white handkerchiefs and upon the dark skirts of women. They were reported on the trees, on the stones, and on the serra. People wept and prayed because of the miracle they had experienced."

A Prayer to Mary

To end, a prayer to Mary:

My Queen, most kind, my hope, O God-Bearer,
refuge for those who are lost and sure defense of travelers,
joy of the sorrowful and suffering,
protectress, you see my need,
you understand my dilemma.
Help me, weak as I am, lead me, a traveler.
Tend to my pain, free me from it,
if you will.
For I have no other helper,
no other protectress, no other kind comforter,
only you, O God-Bearer,
to preserve and protect me world without end. Amen.

From the *Prayers for the Feast Day of the Smolenskaya Icon*.

Acknowledgements

Cover: *Renaissance Madonna and Child*; Ali Meyer/Corbis.

Page 4: *Mary and the Evangelist John* (detail); National Gallery, Sofia.

Page 6: *The Virgin and the Child* (detail) by Duccio; National Gallery, London.

Page 9: *Madonna & Child Surrounded by Angels*, The Wilton Diptych; National Gallery, London.

Page 10: *The Mother of God of the Burning Bush* by Eduard Gubelin; Photo Perret, Lucerne.

Page 12: *The Virgin Mary* by Jean-Loup Charmet.

Page 14: *The Annunciation* by Duccio; National Gallery, London.

Page 17: *Angel Appearing to Joseph*; Musee Conde, Chantilly.

Page 18: *Angel Appearing to Zacharias*; Wildenstein Collection.

Page 21: *Meeting of Joachim and Anne* by Bernardo Daddi; Uffizi Gallery, Florence.

Page 22: *Elisabeth and Mary* by Master of Charles V; The Arenberg Missal.

Page 25: *The Virgin Annunciate* by Naddo Ceccarelli; Noortman (London) Ltd.

Page 26: *The Birth of the Baptist* by Pontormo; Uffizi Gallery, Florence.

Page 29: *La Nativita*; National Gallery of Art, Washington D.C.

Page 30: *A Savior is Born in the City of David*; National Library, Paris.

Page 33: *The Presentation of Jesus in the Temple* by Govanni Bellini; Galleria Querini-Stampalia, Venice.

Page 34: *Adoration of the Magi* by Lorenzo Monaco; Uffizi Gallery, Florence.

Page 37: *The Holy Family on Their Way to Egypt*; National Library, Paris.

Page 38: *Christ Discovered in the Temple* by Simone Martini; Walker Art Gallery, Liverpool.

Page 40: *The Baptism of Christ* by Fra Angelico; Museo di San Marco dell'Angelico, Florence.

Page 43: *John the Forerunner* by Yaroslavl; The Tretiakov Gallery, Moscow.

Page 45: *Wedding at Cana* by Giotto; Scrovegni Chapel, Padua.

Page 46: *Christ Teaching in the Temple* by Fra Angelico; Convent of San Marco, Florence.

Page 49: *Dispute with the Doctors* by Taddeo Gaddi; Scala Photographic Institute, Florence.

Page 50: *Crucifixion*; Saint Catherine's Monastery, Sinai.

Page 52: *All Creation Rejoices in Christ* by School of Dionissi; Tretyakov Gallery, Moscow.

Page 55: *The Ark of the Covenant: David's War and His Coronation*; The Art Archive.

Page 57: *The Temple in Jerusalem* by Aguste Calmet; © Bojan Brecelj.

Page 58: *The Raising of the Ark of the Covenant*; The Art Archive.

Page 61: *Mother of God* by Bogolyubskaya with Zosima and Savaty of Slovek; Photo Perret, Lucerne.

Page 62: *The Burning Bush* by Nicolas Froment; Cathedral Saint-Sauveur, Aix-en-Provence.

Page 65: *The Tree of Jesse*; Richardson & Kailas Icons, London.

Page 66: *Adoration of the Child* by Fra Filippo Lippi; Uffizi Gallery, Florence.

Page 69: *Saints Anna and Joachim*; Ciobanu Collection, Buchrist.

Page 70: *Presentation of the Virgin in the Temple* by Prato Master; Scala Photographic Institute, Florence.

Page 72: *Coronation of the Virgin* by Fra Angelico; Uffizi Gallery, Florence.

Page 75: *The Virgin and the Child*; Church of Saint John the Baptist, Fladbury.

Page 76: *Madonna and Child in a Rosary* by the Savoy School; National Gallery of Art, Washington D.C.

Page 80: *Madonna & Child* by Domnico Veneziano; Villa I Tatti, Settignano.

Page 83: *Our Lady of Vladimir* by Simon Ushakov; Tretyakov Gallery, Moscow.

Page 84: *Nativity* by Simone dei Crocifissi; Uffizi Gallery, Florence.

Page 86: *The Avignon Pieta* attributed to Enguerrand Quarton; Musee du Louvre, Paris.

Page 88: *Coronation of the Virgin* (detail) by Fra Angelico; Uffizi Gallery, Florence.

Page 91: *Transfiguration*; Saint Catherine's Monastery, Sinai.

Page 92: *Madonna and Child Enthroned* by Margarito d'Arezzo; National Gallery of Art, Washington D.C.

Page 95: *Saint Mark's Sacristy* by Melozzo da Forli; Vatican Museums, Rome.

Page 96: *Our Lady of Victory of Malega* by Luis Nino; Denver Art Museum, Denver.

Page 99: *The Dormition of the Virgin* by Theophanes the Greek; Tretyakov Gallery, Moscow.

Page 100: *The Virign* by Joseph Stell; Brooklyn Museum, Brooklyn.

Page 103: *Our Lady: The Enclosed Garden* by Nikita Pavlovets; Tretyakov Gallery, Moscow.

Page 104: *Madonna in the Rose Garden* by Stefan Lochner; Scala / Art Resource.

Page 107: *The Annunciation* by Simone Martini and Lippo Memmi; Uffizi Gallery, Florence.

Page 109: *The Mother of God*; Archive for Art & History, Berlin.

Page 110: *The Unsleeping Eye* by Moscow School; Icon Museum, Racklinghausen.

Page 113: *Our Lady Mary with Her Beloved Son*; Institute of Ethiopian Studies, Addis Ababa.

Page 114: *Saint Paraskyeva-Pyatnitsa*; Korin Collection, Moscow.

Page 116: *Notre Dame de Lourdes* by Justin Pibou; © Iain Pears.

Page 119: *Maria Aparencia al Gruta de Lourdes*; Uffizi and Pitti Galleries, Florence.

Page 120: *Icon with the Virign and Saint John*; National Gallery, Sofia.

Page 123: *Our Lady of Walsingham*; The Anglican Shrine.

Page 124: *Scenes From the Life of Elijah*; The Art Archive.

Page 127: *Our Lady of Mt. Carmel* by Mario Parial; Dr. & Mrs. Yolando Sulit Collection.

Page 128: *Our Lady of Czestochowa* attributed to St. Luke; Art Resource, New York.

Page 131: *The Evangelist Luke as Portrait Painter of the Mother of God*; Archive for Art and History, Berlin.

Page 132: *Our Lady of Guadalupe* by Rufino Tamayo; Mary-Anne Martin Fine Arts, New York.

Page 136: *Bernadette Bergere* by Laugee & Jhenne; Notre-Dame de Lourdes, Paris.

Page 139: *The Grotto of Massabieille*; Mary Evans Picture Library, London.

Page 140: *The Virgin and Child* from an Ethopian Coptic icon; Richardson and Kailas Icons, London.

Page 144: *Coronation of the Virgin*, Bolivia; Uffizi and Pitti Galleries, Florence.

Page 147: *Virgin of the Apocalypse* by workshop of the Master of the Amsterdam Cabinet, Upper Rhine; Metropolitan Museum of Art, New York.

Page 148: *The Mother of God of Yaroslavl*; Icon Museum, Racklinghausen.